TIP 2 **Support your child as he/she reads the story pages:**

• give the book to your child to read and turn the pages.

• where necessary, encourage your child to break a word into syllables, sound out each one, and then flow the syllables together. Ask him/her to reread the sentence to check the meaning.

• when there's a question mark or an exclamation mark, encourage your child to vary his/her voice as he/she reads the sentence. Demonstrate how to do this if it is helpful.

TIP 3 **Chat at the end of each page:**

• ask questions about the text and the meaning of the words used. These help to develop comprehension skills and awareness of the language used.

A FEW ADDITIONAL TIPS

• Always encourage your child to try reading difficult words by themselves. Praise any self-corrections, for example, "I like the way you sounded out that word and then changed the way you said it, to make sense."

• Try to read together everyday. Reading little and often is best. These books are divided into manageable chapters for one reading session. However, after 10 minutes, only keep going if your child wants to read on.

• Read other books of different types to your child just for enjoyment and information.

Series consultant, **Dr. Linda Gambrell**, Distinguished Professor of Education at Clemson University, has served as President of the National Reading Conference, the College Reading Association, and the International Reading Association.

Penguin
Random
House

For Dorling Kindersley
Editors Ellie Barton, Elizabeth Dowsett,
Natalie Edwards, Matt Jones, Clare Millar
Senior Slipcase Designer Mark Penfound
Senior Designer David McDonald
Design Managers Guy Harvey,
Ron Stobbart
Jacket Design Mabel Chan
Pre-Production Producer Kavita Varma
Producer Isobel Reid
Managing Editor Catherine Saunders
Design Manager Guy Harvey
Creative Manager Sarah Harland
Publisher Julie Ferris
Art Director Lisa Lanzarini
Publishing Director Simon Beecroft

For Lucasfilm
Assistant Editor Samantha Holland
Image Archives Newell Todd,
Gabrielle Levenson
Art Director Troy Alders
Story Group Leland Chee, Pablo Hildalgo,
Matt Martin

Designed and edited by Tall Tree Ltd
Designer Ben Ruocco
Editor Jon Richards

This edition published in 2017
First American Edition, 2016
Published in the United States by DK Publishing
345 Hudson Street, New York, New York 10014
DK, a Division of Penguin Random House LLC

Page design copyright © 2017 Dorling
Kindersley Limited

Slipcase UID: 001-309485-Dec/2017

© & TM 2017 LUCASFILM LTD.

A catalog record for this book is available from
the Library of Congress.

ISBN: 978-0-7566-6691-0

Printed and bound in China

www.dk.com
www.starwars.com

A WORLD OF IDEAS:
SEE ALL THERE IS TO KNOW

Contents

STAR WARS™

CLONE TROOPERS IN ACTION

Written by Clare Hibbert

What a huge army! These soldiers are clone troopers. Every soldier is the same. The soldiers are human, but they wear armor that makes them look like robots.

The troopers fight
for the Republic.
So do the Jedi.

The Jedi

The Jedi are warriors
who fight for good.
Not all of the Jedi are
human. They are many
different creatures.

Obi-Wan Kenobi was the first
Jedi to see the clone troopers.
He discovered the army on a
planet near the edge of the galaxy.
This planet is called Kamino.

Obi-Wan Kenobi

Obi-Wan Kenobi is a
Jedi Master. A Jedi
Master is a high-
ranking Jedi who has
carried out many brave
acts. Obi-Wan is very
skilled at fighting with
his lightsaber.

This is Jango Fett. He is very good at fighting. All the clone troopers are copies of Jango. Scientists made the clone babies and grew them inside glass jars. The babies will grow into troopers.

Clones

Clones are exact copies of living things. Thousands of clones of Jango Fett have been made to create the clone army.

The clones are off to fight their first
battle. They fly to the battle inside
huge warships. Jedi Master Yoda
flies with them. He is a very wise
Jedi. He is hundreds of years old.

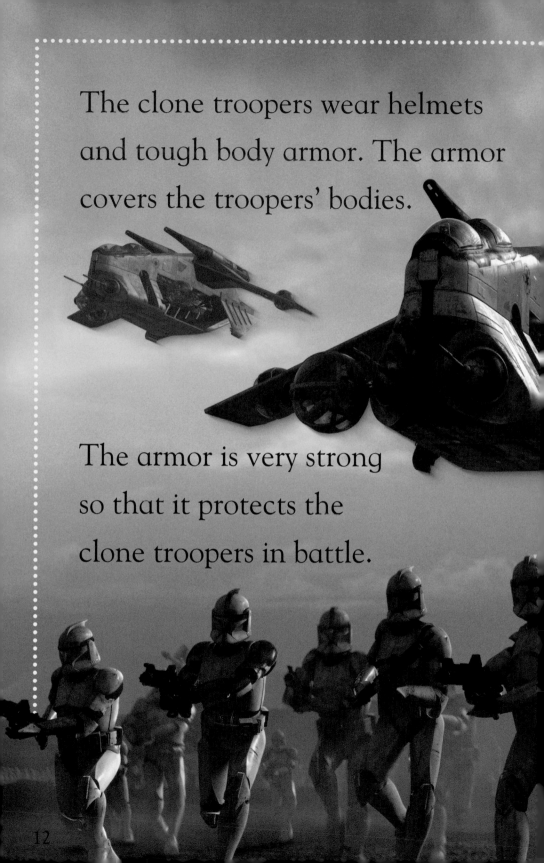

The clone troopers wear helmets and tough body armor. The armor covers the troopers' bodies.

The armor is very strong so that it protects the clone troopers in battle.

Officers

Clone officers wear blue, green, red, or yellow stripes on their armor. Yellow is for the highest rank— clone commander.

Zoom! These clone troopers are driving speeder bikes. The bikes fly high above the ground.

They are super-fast and are used
to soar above a planet's surface.
The bikes have blaster cannons
to fire at enemies.

This is an even faster way to travel! This starfighter is flown by a clone pilot. Starfighters are small and fast ships. They are often launched from larger ships to attack the enemy.

Clone pilots

Just like the clone troopers, clone pilots are
exact copies of Jango Fett.

Oh no! These clone troopers are attacking a Jedi. What is going on? Chancellor Palpatine has told everyone that the Jedi are bad. He orders the clone troopers to attack the Jedi suddenly so that the Jedi can't fight back.

Evil leader

Chancellor Palpatine is hungry for power. He pretends to be good, but he will stop at nothing to take control of the whole galaxy.

Now the troopers are called stormtroopers. They don't fight with the Jedi. They fight against them. The stormtroopers obey Palpatine and his second-in-command, Darth Vader. Palpatine is now called the Emperor and he rules the galaxy.

Darth Vader

Darth Vader
is part-human
and part-machine.
He was once a Jedi
Knight called Anakin
Skywalker, but now he
has turned to evil.

Some stormtroopers have special jobs. Scout troopers check out enemy territory. Snowtroopers fight on icy worlds. No matter what their job, all stormtroopers are well known for one thing—they always follow orders!

Scout
trooper

Snowtrooper

This tall walking tank is called an AT-AT. It carries stormtroopers into battle.
They are looking for Princess Leia and the secret Rebel base on an icy planet called Hoth.
Quick! Stop those walkers!

Rebels
The Rebel Alliance is fighting against Emperor Palpatine and the stormtroopers. Princess Leia is one of the Rebel commanders.

Stormtroopers are strong, but they are no match for Chewbacca. Get them, Chewie! Wait! These aren't stormtroopers!

Luke and his friend Han Solo
are wearing stormtrooper armor
as a disguise!

These stormtroopers are on a very large spaceship called the Death Star. They are guarding the Death Star from any Rebel attacks.

Death Star

The Death Star is shaped like an enormous ball. It is powerful enough to destroy an entire planet!

Can Luke, Han, and Leia defeat the stormtroopers and destroy the Death Star?

Hurray! Luke and his
friends Han, Chewie, and
Leia have helped the Rebels
destroy the Death Star.
But what will happen to the
stormtroopers?
Will they rise again to fight
the valiant Rebels?

Quiz

1. Are clone troopers robots?

2. Who was cloned to make the troopers?

3. Where were the first clone troopers from?

4. What rank is this yellow clone trooper?

5. Who is this Rebel commander ?

6. Who gives orders to the stormtroopers?

Answers: 1. No, they are humans. 2. Jango Fett, a bounty hunter. 3. The planet Kamino. 4. Commander. 5. Princess Leia. 6. Darth Vader and Palpatine.